The Last Duel

by

Martyn Beardsley

Illustrated by Kevin Hopgood

To my daughter Evie, who's certainly
worth fighting a duel over!

Kevin Hopgood

First published in 2007 in Great Britain by
Barrington Stoke Ltd
18 Walker St, Edinburgh EH3 7LP

www.barringtonstoke.co.uk

Copyright © 2007 Martyn Beardsley
Illustrations © Kevin Hopgood

The moral right of the author has been asserted in
accordance with the Copyright, Designs and
Patents Act 1988

ISBN 978-1-84299-455-9

Printed in Great Britain by Bell & Bain Ltd

Contents

Prologue
Portsmouth, 20th May 1845

At around six o'clock in the evening, four men made their way to the seashore. They stopped at a place where the steep beach sloped up away from the sea, forming a long ridge. Here, they could not be seen by people further inland. It was a warm spring evening. The orange sun was sinking towards the gently lapping grey sea, but there was still plenty of daylight left.

One of the men carried a parcel under his arm. Now he began to unwrap the brown paper. Inside was a wooden box. He opened the box, took out one of two pistols which were inside, and began to load it.

The two other men were standing a little way away. They had a box too. They were also loading their pistols.

When everything was ready, the man who had loaded the first pistol walked to a clear, level spot on the beach and drew a line in the pebbles with his shoe. He then walked slowly forwards. After twelve paces he stopped, and made another mark.

He looked up and spoke to the two men who were now holding the loaded guns. He took a deep breath and said in a loud, clear voice:

"Gentlemen, it is time to go to your marks and await my signal."

The two men kept their pistols pointing down, as they walked slowly to their places, their feet scrunching through the pebbles. Then they stopped and turned to face each other with their guns by their sides, and waited in silence. The only sounds came from the waves washing up the beach, and the cry of a lone seagull circling above them.

"Are you ready, gentlemen?"

Both nodded.

There was a short pause, then:

"FIRE!"

An old Royal Navy carpenter was taking a stroll close to the beach when he heard shots ring out. The sounds seemed quite close, but when he stopped to look round he could see no one. Soon, however, a man came running towards him from the direction of the shots. He was out of breath and looked worried.

"Can you tell me where I can get a doctor?" cried the man.

"What's happened?" the carpenter asked.

"A man is very ill on the beach," was all the man would say.

The carpenter told him where to go, and the man ran off as fast as he could.

Moments later, the carpenter met two more running men. But these two did not stop. They were dressed in black, and turned their faces away from him as they passed. One of them was carrying something wrapped in a cloth. They vanished in the direction of the next village, and the carpenter never saw them again.

Chapter 1

The History of Duelling

You have found the secret of time travel, and you decide to see what life was like two hundred years ago.

It is amazing! Everything is so different – the houses, the roads, the way people speak, the clothes they wear. But you remember you are still wearing your jeans and t-shirt and everyone is looking at you. You see a very splendid uniform in a shop –

it fits perfectly, and you decide to buy it. You don't know it but everyone else now thinks that you are an army officer!

A man and a woman come towards you along the pavement. He is also wearing a uniform, but it is a different colour from yours. The street is very busy and crowded. As they walk past you, another man in a great hurry pushes between you and the woman, and she is knocked over. She had been looking away and didn't see the other man – she bursts into tears and blames you!

The army officer with her demands that you apologise for knocking his wife over. He calls you a clumsy fool. Now you are angry – the woman is quite wrong, and anyway you are *not* a clumsy fool. You are not going to apologise for something you didn't do! By now, a crowd is gathering.

Now the army man says in a loud voice that if you won't apologise for what you have done, he demands to meet you with pistols on Maybury Hill at dawn.

You hear a whisper in your ear and turn. There are two men wearing the same uniform as you. One of them is telling you that he saw it all and he knows that you did not do it – but now it's too late. You must accept the challenge. If you refuse you will look like a coward in front of all these people. You will be letting yourself and the army down. There is no choice, he tells you.

At first, you are not too worried. The time travelling device is in your pocket and by pressing a button you could simply return to your own time and forget it all. But everyone is looking at you, waiting to see what you are going to do, and suddenly it is not such an easy decision. You have

been insulted in public. They are waiting to see if you are a coward, or a person of courage and honour.

Then you think about what it will be like if you accept his challenge to a duel. Unlike you, he is a proper soldier, trained to shoot a gun, trained to kill. You have never even held a real gun in your hand before! You think of the sleepless night of worry. You think of rising very early and making your lonely way to Maybury Hill in the cold morning air. You see yourself standing a few paces away from his sneering face, staring down the barrel of his pistol, waiting for the signal to fire.

What kind of pain do you feel when a bullet cuts through your flesh, bounces off bone, smashes through anything in its path inside your body in the blink of an eye, and comes out on the other side?

You have to make up your mind. The crowd has grown bigger, and they are waiting …

Duelling of one sort or another is probably as old as mankind. Since the start of the human race, people have wanted to test themselves against each other to see who is the fastest, the strongest, the better fighter. Fighting could be anything from large groups of people going to war to just two people losing their tempers.

Duelling is indeed a sort of fighting, but with a difference. It is not when two men suddenly get angry and start to fight.
A duel is planned in advance and there are rules about how it must be fought. One of the ideas behind this was to turn what might be a fight to the death into as controlled an event as possible. A place and time was set. They had to follow rules and there had to be people there to witness

it. All this helped to make things as fair as could be.

Any fight arranged in advance between two people could loosely be called a duel. By the time our story was set, in 1845, and for a hundred years or more before, the word had begun to mean something more.

There were two very important things that set a duel apart from other kinds of fighting.

For one thing, it was only considered a duel if it involved *gentlemen*. That word had a different meaning in 1845 from the way we understand it now. A gentleman was a man in the higher levels of society. A farm worker, a baker or a shopkeeper, no matter how well behaved or how perfect his manners, was not thought of as a gentleman. Most rich men, lords and land-owners were always thought of as gentlemen.

One of the few ways a man might move "up" and become a gentleman was to become an officer in the army, navy or the marines. Such an officer was almost always looked upon as a gentleman. If he hadn't been one before, he might have to learn to dress and behave like a gentleman in society.

The other aspect of duelling was that it had to be fought over a matter of *honour*. It is very difficult to describe exactly what that was, because it meant very different things to different people even then. In some cases duels were fought over what look like very small arguments.

In one case, a soldier called Campbell gave an order to the men on parade. His General said the order was wrong. Later, at dinner, Campbell and a friend called Boyd argued over whether or not he had given the correct order. Campbell became very angry. He felt that he was made to look like a bad officer and because of this he had to "defend his honour". They met in a duel, and Campbell shot Boyd dead.

It was very risky to insult a military officer!

There were no actual written rules for duelling but over the years an idea of what should be done had developed. This started from well before a shot was fired. Firstly, you were seen to be a coward if you refused a challenge, no matter how stupid or small the argument, or how wrong the other person was. Once the challenge had been made, a man would be seen as a coward if he refused to meet his opponent "in the field" as it was known. An army officer refusing a duel could expect to become an outcast, with fellow officers refusing to talk to him because his cowardly action had made his whole regiment look bad.

To plan the duel, the fighters each chose a "second" to act for him from the start. (The term "second" is still used in boxing for someone looking after the fighter in his corner.) Most often the "second", not the duellist, would give the challenge – sometimes in the form of a letter or card. Most of the time the person being challenged decided on the place, time and weapons to be used. The place was most often somewhere they were unlikely to be seen or arrested. And the weapons used by this time were almost always pistols (swords were now old-fashioned).

Unlike gunfights in cowboy films, there was no attempt at a "quick draw" in a duel. One of the seconds gave the command, and both duellists raised their pistols at the same time. People even thought it unsporting to take very careful aim in the way you would when shooting at a target. You were expected to raise, point, and fire.

Quite often one man would get his shot in first and aim very high or wide so that it was clear to his opponent that he intended to miss. This might happen if, for example, having had time to cool down he no longer wanted to kill someone over some silly argument. In this case, the other man would also decide to miss on purpose. Because they had both been brave enough to take part in the duel, fully expecting to risk their lives, they could leave the field with their honour unharmed.

When you see people in films and TV shooting guns they often hold their gun with both hands and stand face-on to their enemy. But in duelling the method was to stand sideways on, holding the pistol in one hand. Standing sideways meant that there was a thinner target to aim at, and that your shooting arm gave some protection to your upper body. The downside of this was that if a pistol ball (bullet) did enter your body from the side, it was likely to pass through more than one vital organ. In fact, the pistols used then were not as accurate as the guns of today, and not many people who took part in duels were killed.

Duelling had been against the law for hundreds of years, and killing someone in a duel was thought of as murder just like any other killing. But there was for a long time a feeling that a gentleman who had been insulted *must* defend his honour, and only a small number of people who were arrested were found guilty by juries in court.

But slowly, attitudes began to change. By 1845 duelling was no longer in fashion and those who took part in duels were more likely to be punished. If you shot someone in a duel you had to either face arrest and maybe a death sentence – or make a run for it.

Chapter 2
Officers and Gentlemen

Henry Hawkey was a big, tough man – someone not to be messed with. He was born a few years after Nelson had defeated the French and Spanish at the Battle of Trafalgar. Hawkey became an officer in the Royal Marines. People said that he had already fought at least one man in a duel in the past.

The Royal Marines sailed on warships (which in those days were made of wood and powered by sail) but they were not sailors. They dressed differently – instead of the blue of the navy, they wore red coats like soldiers. They were there to help keep order on board ship. For example, they stood outside the captain's cabin to protect him, and kept order when sailors were flogged for breaking the ship's rules. In battle they fired on the enemy with their muskets. Some helped to work the big cannon, and some formed groups ready to try to get on board the enemy ship if it came close enough – or to stop the enemy from getting on to their own ship.

Britain was no longer at war when Hawkey joined the Marines. He spent much of his time ashore, moving between the Royal Marine bases along the south coast of England. This meant that when his day's work was done, he was often free to go home to his wife Isabella.

Every week when they were in Portsmouth they liked to go dancing at the King's Rooms. This was a very popular place, and a lot of military people went there. Portsmouth was full of sailors, marines, and soldiers, but only the officers enjoyed places like the King's Rooms. The ordinary soldiers and sailors would never have been allowed in, and wouldn't have wanted to go anyway. They would go to one of the many pubs and inns all over town, where they could have a good time without having to wear fancy clothes and behave nicely.

But for once, even the King's Rooms was about to witness "behaviour unbecoming an officer and a gentleman" (the words used when an officer behaved badly). This was because on the night before the duel, another man entered the Rooms – a man who knew and liked Lieutenant Hawkey and his wife Isabella. At least, he liked Isabella. He liked her a lot.

Chapter 3
An Unwanted Visitor

James Seton had served in the army. He was a cavalry officer, and he liked to boast about it. "James Seton, late of the 11th Hussars" sounded good. But he had in fact only spent a year with the Hussars, and doesn't seem to have done very much during that time. Since leaving the army he had got quite fat.

Seton was married, so it's odd that he should have been so interested in Isabella. Perhaps he never really loved his wife. In those days people from rich families tended to think that it was important to marry someone from the "right sort" of background who had the right amount of money. Often – though not always – love came second to this, if it came in at all.

Whatever the reason, James Seton had been showing a lot of interest in Isabella.

They had first met during a ball at the King's Rooms, some weeks before the duel. Hawkey introduced his new friend Seton to his wife, and Seton and Isabella danced together. They bumped into each other a few times after this. Seton began to change the way he acted around her. He wanted her to be his girlfriend – even though they were both married.

Once he visited Isabella when Hawkey was out. Seton spent some time talking to her until, feeling this was wrong, Isabella looked at the clock and said, "I believe your wife will be wondering where you have got to, Mr Seton."

He just smiled at her and said, "I don't care!"

Another time she met Seton and his wife when they were out walking with friends. Seton came up to her and asked her to take his arm while they walked.

"I think it would be better if I did not," said Isabella.

"If one lady takes it, another may," insisted Seton. "You see my wife is walking with a friend of ours."

"I'm afraid my husband wouldn't like it."

Some time later he gave her a bunch of flowers, and then he visited her when he knew her husband would be at drill with the Marines.

"Let's speak plainly," Seton said. "Are you interested in me or not? I know Hawkey has a hot temper, and if he finds out about us I shall have to go out with him in the end." By 'going out', Seton meant fighting a duel. "But it would be worth it for you, Isabella," he added.

But while he was talking so bravely a knock came at the door, and Seton cried, "Good God, here's Hawkey!" He ran to get his hat from the table, begging, "Can't you let me out?"

He was lucky this time, for it was Hawkey's friend Lieutenant Pym who was at the door, not Hawkey himself.

But this scare didn't put Seton off.

A few days later he met Isabella again and tried to give her a beautiful and expensive ring.

"You know I cannot take this, Mr Seton," said Isabella.

"Perhaps you want more? I once gave a lady £1,000 worth of jewellery. Might something like that make you more interested in me?"

"Please do not insult me any more by such offers, sir," said Isabella firmly.

"If that's your attitude, a man has no chance!" said Seton.

"But you are a *married* man!"

"I don't care about my wife, nor she about me. We both please ourselves, my dear."

"Well, I do care, sir, and if you insist like this I shall go home to my mother and you shall see me no more."

Isabella didn't tell Hawkey about Seton, fearing that his temper would get the better of him and there would be trouble. But she was upset and had to tell someone. Isabella turned to their friend Pym, who was like a brother to her and her husband. But Pym felt he had to warn his friend Hawkey about what was going on.

Hawkey was annoyed that Isabella hadn't told him what Seton had been up to, but he promised her that if she would just give him all the details the matter would end there. This could have been the end of it all – but Seton was not going to let the matter stop there.

Chapter 4

Trouble at the King's Rooms

There was a ball at the King's Rooms on the evening of Monday the 19th of May. Before all the trouble had started, Isabella had promised Seton that she would have one dance with him on this evening. Now, of course, she didn't want to. Hawkey said that a promise was a promise, and that she should dance with him – but in a dance called a "quadrille", where the partners were further apart from each other than in some other dances.

The mood between the Hawkeys and the Setons at the ball was tense, but Isabella danced her dance with Seton. By now, however, his feelings about fighting a duel with Hawkey had changed. He told Isabella, "I will not go out with him. It wouldn't be right for a light cavalry man to duel with a mere infantry man."

This seems to be a rule that Seton had made up to suit himself. Perhaps he had heard the story that Hawkey had already faced up to other men with the pistols and lived to tell the tale.

When the dance was over, Isabella sat down and Seton sat next to her. Hawkey came over to them and asked to sit next to his wife. When Seton refused to move, this was the last straw.

"Sir, I should like to have a few words with you in a private room," Hawkey growled.

"That is what I wish myself," Seton replied.

The two men went into an empty room away from the dancing which was sometimes used for card games. No one went in with them, and no one would ever know what they said to each other. But there was a serious argument, because as soon as Seton came out he went up to Isabella with a worried look on his face.

"For God's sake, sort this out with your husband or the whole world will be talking about us!" he begged her.

But Isabella wanted no more to do with him. She found Lieutenant Pym, who took her home.

When Seton left he had to pass Hawkey, who was in a chair by the door. There was more arguing, and Seton repeated his claim that a light cavalry man could not duel with an infantry man. Saying it to Hawkey's face was almost the same as saying that a Royal Marine officer was not good enough to challenge him to a duel. This insult made Hawkey wild with anger.

He kicked out at Seton as he passed, saying, "Sir, you are a blackguard and a scoundrel." (Those were the worst insults you could use to an officer!) "And if you won't fight me," Hawkey went on, "I'll horsewhip you up and down the High Street!"

Seton stormed past him and out of the King's Rooms. But it wasn't the last Hawkey had heard of him.

Chapter 5

I'll Shoot Him Like a Partridge!

Early the next morning, while Hawkey was still in bed, there was a knock at the door. It turned out to be a Lieutenant Rowles of the Royal Navy with a very important message from his friend, Seton.

Lieutenant Rowles was very polite, but the message he had come to deliver would change all of their lives. Seton was challenging Hawkey to a duel. Seton might have wanted to talk his way out of such a risky step, but Hawkey had insulted him in front of too many people last night. No matter how afraid he felt, he had to challenge Hawkey or risk being called a coward.

Hawkey wanted to fight Seton. He was overheard telling Pym, "I'll shoot him like a partridge!"

They visited Mr Field's gun shop. Hawkey wanted to see some of his pistols. He saw a pair with nine-inch barrels (about 22 centimetres long) and hair triggers (which need very little squeezing to make the gun fire).

"These look a fine pair," said Hawkey. "Just the sort I need."

"May I ask what you need them for, sir?" asked Mr Field.

"Oh, I'm having a shooting match with Pym – the winner gets five shillings! May I borrow these?"

Mr Field said, "They're brand new so I'm afraid I can't lend them out. But you can buy them if you wish."

"I shall take them down to Sherwood's shooting gallery to try them out," Hawkey told him.

"Then I'm sure Mr Sherwood will have some that you can borrow, rather than buying new ones."

"He has none good enough for what I want," came Hawkey's reply.

Soon afterwards, Hawkey and Pym arrived at Sherwood's shooting gallery. Hawkey was seen measuring out twelve paces from the target before starting his practice. Twelve paces just so happened to be a standard distance used for duelling.

After his last shot Hawkey walked up to the target to examine the hole, and said, "*That* would have done him!"

Later on in the afternoon, Pym ordered his servant to follow him down to the water's edge, where they took a short boat trip across to Gosport. Pym gave his servant a parcel to carry – it was wrapped in brown paper and felt hard, as if made of wood, but he didn't tell the servant what was in it. After walking through the centre of Gosport they arrived near the beach and met Hawkey. Pym now took the parcel, told his man to wait there, and the two walked away until they had vanished over a ridge in the pebble beach.

And so it was that Lieutenant Hawkey and his second, Lieutenant Pym, arrived at

the chosen place for the duel. It was at a place called Browndown, not far from the Preventive Station which kept a watch out for smugglers on that part of the coast.

Seton and his second, Lieutenant Rowles, were there waiting for them. The duelling ground was marked out, and each duellist chose a pistol from the pair presented to him. Hawkey had scratched a cross on the one which he thought was the better gun.

On the command, Hawkey and Seton took up their positions twelve paces apart, trying their best to steady their nerves and stop their hands from shaking. The order to fire was given. They raised their pistols and squeezed the triggers.

There was a flash, a loud crack, and a puff of smoke. A smell of gunpowder, all too familiar to the military men present, drifted on the breeze. But it came from only one of the pistols.

One gun had failed to go off.

Chapter 6
An Unfair Contest

Pym had not prepared Hawkey's pistol properly, a mistake which could have cost his friend his life.

The kind of gun in use then had a small hammer on top, just above the thumb, which was pulled back and clicked into place. When the trigger was pulled, the hammer shot forwards, making a spark which ignited the gunpowder and fired the bullet.

But before the hammer, or cock, was pulled fully back there was a half-way position into which it could be clicked. The gun could be safely left like this before firing, because the hammer could not travel far enough to cause a spark and fire the bullet. Hawkey's gun seems to have gone off at this "half-cock" position. This is a saying we still use today when a person starts doing something before they are fully ready.

When he heard the bang from Seton's pistol and found that his own had not fired, Hawkey must have frozen with horror for a moment, expecting to feel the pain from Seton's bullet as it thudded into his body. But Seton missed.

Under the rules of duelling, this should have been the end of the duel. Seton was the challenger. He had shot and missed, and he should have considered his honour satisfied. But Seton was not satisfied.

Whether it was because he was afraid of not settling the matter and still being seen as a coward, or whether he really wanted to hurt Hawkey, he asked for the second pistols to be fetched. Now it was the other second's turn to make a mistake. Rowles obeyed Seton and fetched the second pistol. Under the rules of duelling he should have refused to do what Seton asked and declared the matter settled. Seton would have had to accept this, and no one could have blamed either duellist for leaving the field.

But Rowles brought the second pistol, and Pym had no choice but to do the same –

this time making sure that it was in full working order.

The order to fire was given again, and this time two shots rang out.

Seton missed again – then slumped to the ground clutching his body. Hawkey's ball (bullets at that time were small balls made of lead) had hit Seton in the hip, passed through his lower belly, and come out near the top of his left leg. He was bleeding badly.

Rowles said Hawkey didn't go over to Seton to see how he was, which was what a gentleman should have done. But Hawkey knew that he was bound to end up being arrested and might be sent to prison or even hanged for murder if he was found. He muttered, "I'm off to France," and ran away with Pym.

Chapter 7

This Unfortunate Gentleman

While Hawkey and Pym were making their escape, Seton was taken to a hotel close by where he was looked after by several doctors. (Hospitals then did not have the kind of medical equipment that we have now, so a clean hotel was just as good.)

The duel soon got into the newspapers. It was a big story because duelling had become rare by this time. The local and national papers reported daily on Seton's condition, while at the same time trying to work out why there had been a duel at all. Letters began to appear from friends of both Seton and Hawkey, each side laying the blame on the other man. The Colonel of the Royal Marines at Portsmouth announced that Lieutenants Hawkey and Pym had gone absent without leave and no one knew where they were.

After a time, the doctors began to worry about Seton's chances of ever getting better. In the end they decided they would have to operate on him. This was a very much riskier thing then than now. Afterwards, the Times newspaper reported: "Everything has now been done which human skill could accomplish to save the life of this unfortunate gentleman. The result will be seen in a few days, perhaps sooner."

James Seton, late of the 11th Hussars, died with his family around him two days later – about two weeks after the duel.

It is almost certain that Pym and Hawkey did go to France to avoid arrest. Hawkey's wife Isabella stayed in Portsmouth long enough to write several letters to the newspapers in defence of her husband, and then probably joined him there.

Almost a year after the duel, Edward Pym surprised everyone by turning up and handing himself in. His part in the duel meant that legally he was guilty as Hawkey for the death of Seton. Isabella herself also appeared as a witness at the trial. The only defence that could be argued for Pym was that it was not the shooting that killed

Seton but the operation afterwards, which Pym's lawyers claimed was risky and not needed.

The judge pointed out that the operation was only done because Seton had been shot in the first place. But the jury seemed happy to be presented with any grounds on which they might spare this young officer – who, after all, had not pulled the trigger himself. They found Pym not guilty.

The verdict, said the Times, "was followed by a burst of applause, clapping hands, and huzzas (people shouting, 'Hooray!')."

Once the trial was over, Hawkey also slipped back into Britain. Like Pym, Hawkey gave himself up and stood trial for murder. And although the age of duelling had now all but come to an end, it seems that public sympathy still lay with an officer and gentleman in defending his honour. Like Pym, Hawkey was found not guilty, taken back into the Marines, and even gained promotion.

It seems, though, that his temper could still get the better of him. Seven years after the duel there was a fight near the Woolwich Royal Marine base involving Captain Hawkey, as he now was, and a junior officer. Hawkey was court-martialled and found guilty of violent assault, though not guilty of "conduct unbecoming an officer and gentleman".

Hawkey died in London seven years later after a long illness – the last man ever to take part in a duel in Britain.

Barrington Stoke would like to thank all its readers for commenting on the manuscript before publication and in particular:

Johnny Elder

Sophie Oates Black

Alison Thomas

Conan Fraser

William Brown

Chandni Soneji

Become a Consultant!

Would you like to give us feedback on our titles before they are published? Contact us at the e-mail address below – we'd love to hear from you!

info@barringtonstoke.co.uk
www.barringtonstoke.co.uk

AUTHOR CHECK LIST

Martyn Beardsley

Who would you like to challenge to a duel?

People who swear or drop litter. I see them when I go out shopping and I often feel like challenging them to a duel!

What would be your choice of weapons?

I would have a very long sword, they would have a very short one with a rubber ball stuck on the end.

If you could time travel, what period of history would you like to visit?

I think I'd go for Victorian times. When I was at school I was given the idea that the Victorians were pretty horrible but now I don't think they were any worse than us – in fact, they were much better in many ways.

And what period of history would you least like to live in?

Around 1348 – when the Black Death came to England and everyone started dying. Much too dangerous! And before late Victorian times they had to do operations without sending you to sleep, so I wouldn't want to live that far back.

If you could be a character from history, who would you pick?

I'm a Buddhist and I think the Buddha had things pretty well sorted, so I'll choose him.

ILLUSTRATOR CHECK LIST

Kevin Hopgood

Who would you like to challenge to a duel?

My ten-year-old son Louis. He trashes me at computer games, but in a real life duel maybe I'd have a chance ...

What would be your choice of weapons?

I think it'd have to be something non-lethal for legal reasons, so water pistols would be a good choice. Come to think about it, I tend to lose in water pistol fights as well.

If you could time travel, what period of history would you like to visit?

I'd like to visit ancient Rome. I wouldn't want to be a slave though.

And what period of history would you least like to live in?

London around the time of the Black Death would be fairly grim.

If you could be a character from history, who would you pick?

I'd want to be someone who lived a long uneventful life, when there were no major wars or civil unrest, or nasty plagues. So no one famous.

Try another book in the
REALITY CHECK
series

Crazy Creatures
by Gill Arbuthnott

Dick Turpin: Legends and Lies
by Terry Deary

Escape From Colditz
by Deborah Chancellor

All available from our website:
www.barringtonstoke.co.uk